Aberdeenshire

PREDATOR VS PREY

Wolf vs Elk

Mary Meinking

www.raintreepublishers.co.uk
Visit our website to find out
more information about
Raintree books.

To order:
☎ Phone 0845 6044371
🖷 Fax +44 (0) 1865 312263
🖳 Email myorders@raintreepublishers.co.uk

Customers from outside the UK please telephone +44 1865 312262

Raintree is an imprint of Capstone Global Library Limited,
a company incorporated in England and Wales having its
registered office at 7 Pilgrim Street, London, EC4V 6LB
– Registered company number: 6695582

Edited by Rebecca Rissman, Dan Nunn,
    and Catherine Veitch
Designed by Joanna Hinton Malivoire
Levelling by Jeanne Clidas
Picture research by Hannah Taylor
Production by Victoria Fitzgerald
Originated by Capstone Global Library
Printed and bound in China by CTPS

ISBN 978 1 406 21871 8
14 13 12 11 10
10 9 8 7 6 5 4 3 2 1

British Library Cataloguing in Publication Data
Meinking, Mary.
Wolf vs elk. -- (Predator vs prey)
591.5'3-dc22
A full catalogue record for this book is available from the
British Library.

Acknowledgements
We would like to thank the following for permission
to reproduce photographs: Alamy Images p. 25 (©
Juniors Bildarchiv), ardea.com pp. 4 (© M. Watson), 13
(© M. Watson); Corbis pp. 22 (AllCanadaPhotos.com),
28 (Tom Brakefield); FLPA pp. 10 (Minden Pictures/Chris
Stenger), 11 (Minden Pictures/Donald M. Jones), 14
(Minden Pictures/Tim Fitzharris), 16 (Minden Pictures/
Jasper Doest), 20 (Minden Pictures/Donald M. Jones), 21
(Minden Pictures/Donald M. Jones), 23 (Minden Pictures/
Donald M. Jones), 24 (Minden Pictures/Donald M. Jones),
26 (Minden Pictures/Donald M. Jones); Getty Images p.
15 (Altrendo); istockphoto pp. 6 (© Vladimir Gramagin),
7 (© Tom Tietz); naturepl.com p. 5 (Eric Baccega);
Photolibrary pp. 8 (E.A. Janes), 9 (age fotostock/
Ronald Wittek), 12 (Oxford Scientific/Daniel J. Cox), 19
(Novastock Novastock), 27 (Oxford Scientific/Michael
Leach), 29 (Mauritius/Ronald Wittek); Photoshot pp. 17
(Larry Ditto), 18 (John Shaw).

Cover photographs of a wolf reproduced with permission
of Photolibrary (age fotostock/ Ronald Wittek), and an
elk reproduced with permission of Alamy Images (© Eye
Ubiquitous).

We would like to thank Michael Bright for his invaluable
help in the preparation of this book.

Some words are shown in bold, **like this.** You can find
out what they mean by looking in the glossary.

Contents

Mountain clash

Teeth rip! Hooves crush! Two challengers meet in the snow-topped mountains. Here's a growling hunter, the wolf. It's up against a towering challenger, the elk.

wolf

elk

These animals live in North America's western mountains. Both have strengths that will help them in this battle.

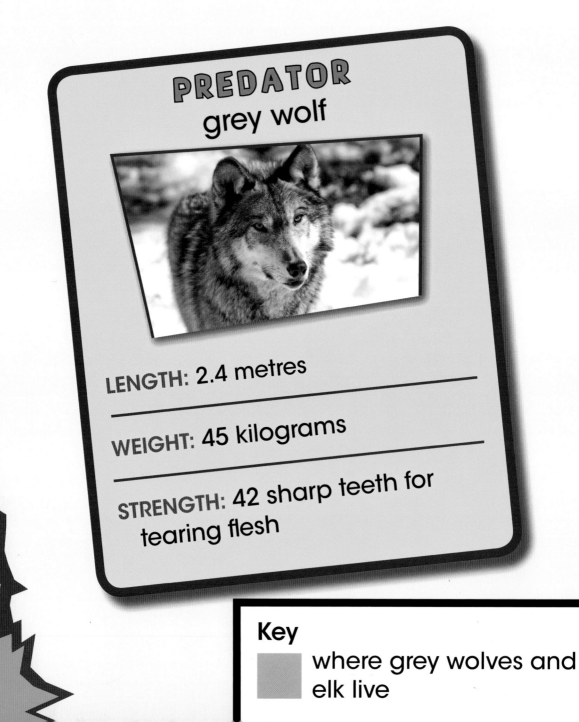

PREDATOR
grey wolf

LENGTH: 2.4 metres

WEIGHT: 45 kilograms

STRENGTH: 42 sharp teeth for tearing flesh

Key

where grey wolves and elk live

PREY
elk

LENGTH: 2.4 metres

WEIGHT: 363 kilograms

STRENGTH: strong legs and hard hooves for kicking

North America

Pack hunters

Wolves hunt in **packs**, or family groups, of six to 12 wolves. Each pack has one wolf that leads them when they are hunting. Wolves catch more **prey** when they work as a team.

DID YOU KNOW?

Wolves have 5-centimetre-long fang-like **canine** teeth. They use these teeth to grab prey. Their back teeth crack the bones.

Hoofing it

The elk has hard hooves. And it is not afraid to use them. If a **predator** gets too close, the elk can kick hard enough to break bones.

DID YOU KNOW?
An elk has a great **sense** of smell. Its nose can sniff out predators nearby.

11

Who's hungry?

Wolves are **carnivores**, or meat eaters. After eating, wolves can go for a week before they need another meal. When they get hungry again, wolves rub noses to tell each other its time to hunt!

13

The hunt

The **herd** of elk is looking for grass to eat. One elk is the lookout, while the others **graze**, or eat. The wolves sniff the air for **prey**. The head male wolf picks up the **scent** of elk. It trots off towards the smell. The other wolves follow behind.

The wolves see the **herd** of elk. They spread out. They creep low and slowly towards the herd. The lookout elk sees something moving in the grass. It's a wolf! The elk "barks" out a warning!

The **pack** of wolves rushes at the **herd** of elk. The elk start running. The wolves are looking for an old, young, ill, or hurt elk. The wolves don't have a chance against a healthy elk. They pick their target.

The wolf **pack** separates a **victim** from the **herd**. They chase it for almost 20 minutes. The elk cannot lose the wolves. It runs into a river. A brave wolf follows the elk. It stops beside the river.

DID YOU KNOW?

Wolves run at 45 kilometres per hour when following **prey**. But elk can run at up to 48 kilometres per hour for a short distance.

When the elk gets tired, it stops and lowers its **antlers** towards the wolf. The wolf leaps into the river. But the elk's not giving up! It kicks at the wolf with its hard hooves. The wolf jumps out of the river.

23

The injured wolf whimpers and backs away. The head wolf keeps trying! But the elk lowers his **antlers** and stabs at the wolf. The wolf backs away and so do the others.

And the winner is...

...the elk! It uses its strong legs to protect itself. Its legs help it to outrun most enemies. If an enemy does corner the elk then its legs give a powerful kick.

What are the odds?

Wolves only catch **prey** once every five tries! They can eat up to 9 kilograms of meat at a time. That's like eating 80 hamburgers! Some of the animals that wolves attack weigh 10 times more than them. Wolves work as a team to bring big prey down.

Glossary

antlers hard, bony growths on a male elk's head

canine long pointed teeth at each side of a wolf's jaws

carnivore animal that eats meat

graze eat grass

herd group of animals living together

pack group of wild animals that hunts and lives together

predator animal that hunts other animals

prey animal that is hunted by other animals for food

scent smell given off by an animal

sense feeling such as sight, hearing, smell, taste, or touch

victim something that suffers because of an action

Find out more

Books

Animal Top Tens: North America's Most Amazing Animals, Anita Ganeri (Raintree Publishers, 2008)

Animals under Threat: Grey Wolf, Jill Bailey (Heinemann, 2005)

Wolf, Michael Leach (Wayland, 2002)

Websites

http://animals.nationalgeographic.com/ animals/mammals/elk.html
Find out more about elk on this website.

http://kids.nationalgeographic.com/ Animals/CreatureFeature/Graywolf
Visit this website to learn more about grey wolves and watch videos of them in the wild.

Index